FOOTBALL TRAINING

FOOTBALL TRAINING

Graham Taylor

LEOPARD

The author and publishers wish to thank Action Images, Action Plus, Allsport and Bob Thomas Sports Photography for permission to reproduce their photographs.

This edition published 1995 by Leopard Books, 20 Vauxhall Bridge Road, London SW1V 2SA

First published 1992 by Stanley Paul & Co. Ltd.

Copyright © 1992 The Football Association

Set in Palatino and Futura

Printed and bound in Great Britain by Scotprint Ltd, Musselburgh

ISBN 0 7529 0126 5

Everybody likes to play, nobody likes to train is the generally held view. This book sets out to explode that myth.

With a series of clearly explained and precisely illustrated exercises, it shows how a training session can be enjoyable as well as constructive, making players fitter, faster and more skilful.

The type of training programme that stands the England team in such good stead can be adapted to the requirements of trainers and managers of young players at all levels. Training can be fun and with the help of this invaluable book, from now on for thousands of players – it will be!

WARM-UP GAMES ▶

These exercises are for a group of 12–14 players.

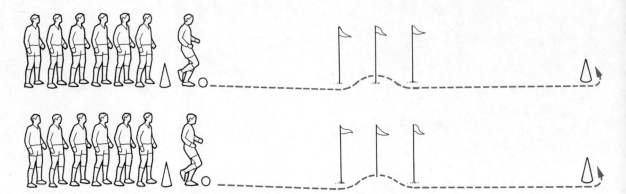

The first player takes the ball on a run, dribbling between the centre sticks and round the end marker. Then he passes back with his right foot for the second player to collect the ball at the start and go on his run.

Variations
1 pass with the left foot
2 use a lofted pass
3 dribble both ways

Two teams in single file face each other, with a small 'goal' between them. Using one ball, the teams pass with one or two touches through the 'goal', with players quickly returning to the back of their own team. Count how many miss the goal and make a competition out of it.

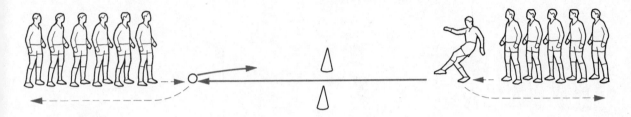

Variations
1 use one foot only to pass
2 players join opposite group – pass and follow

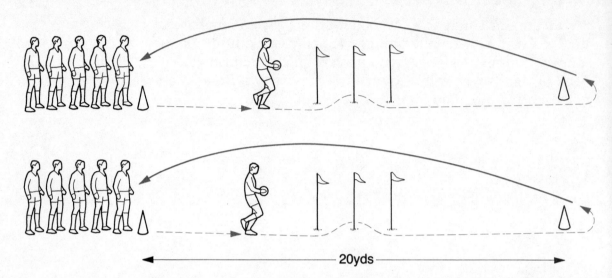

20yds

This uses a 20-yard course with three sticks placed in the centre with one yard between each. The first player holds the ball in his hands and runs in and out of the sticks (without knocking them over), round the end cone and then volleys right-footed for the second player to catch cleanly behind the starter cone. If the ball hits the ground, it is returned to the volleying player to repeat the volley before the second player embarks on his run.

Variations
1 left-foot volley
2 right-foot, half-volley
3 left-foot, half-volley

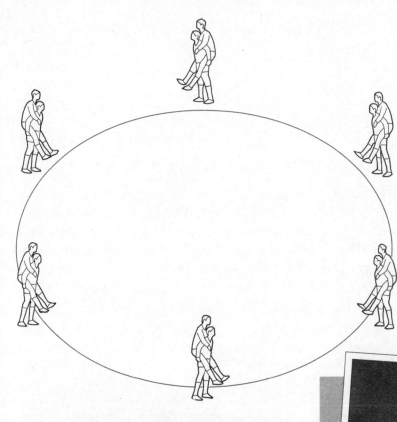

Players gather in piggy-back pairs around the centre circle. Each 'jockey' has to react to instructions made by the coach, e.g. down through the 'horse's' legs, run round the circle and get back onto his partner's back.

The last pair back have to do press-ups as a forfeit. Vary the instruction to keep people thinking.

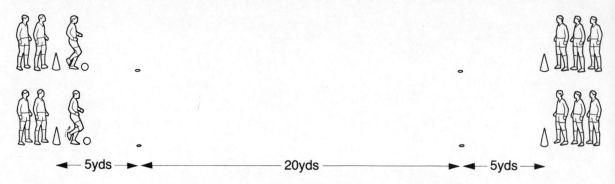

◄— 5yds —► ◄————————— 20yds —————————► ◄— 5yds —►

A straight course is required, 20 yards long, with small five-yard areas each end for change-over. The first player, with ball under control, runs and passes to his partner in the take-over area. Competition continues until each player has returned to the starting position. Play all the games at speed to encourage competition. Press-up forfeit for faults, e.g. dropping the ball or starting too early.

Variations
1 carry the ball and head to partner
2 carry the ball and volley to partner

Two teams of six players each occupy a full-sized pitch. A player has the ball in his hands, throws to a team-mate who must then head the ball to a colleague who must in turn catch or handle the ball and so on.

The sequence of throw-head-catch must be strictly adhered to! To intercept, the opponents must follow the same sequence. Two sequential catches or heads mean a free throw to the other team. This is a hard game for the coach to referee!

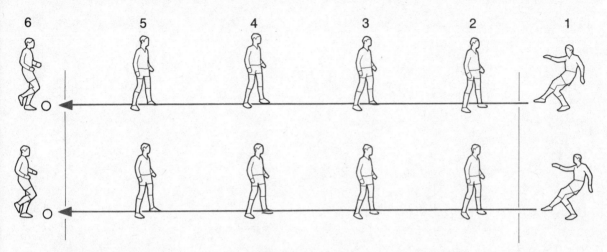

Two teams spread out between two lines, the goal-line and 18-yard area. Starting player (1) passes the ball between the legs of his team-mates to reach player (6) behind the end line. He then has to dribble the ball to the front and repeat, whilst his team shuffles back and player (5) receives a pass.

A competition like this is sure to keep training warm-ups keen!

Variations
1 receiver dribbles in and out of his team
2 pass with the left or right foot only

19

ACROSS THE CIRCLE

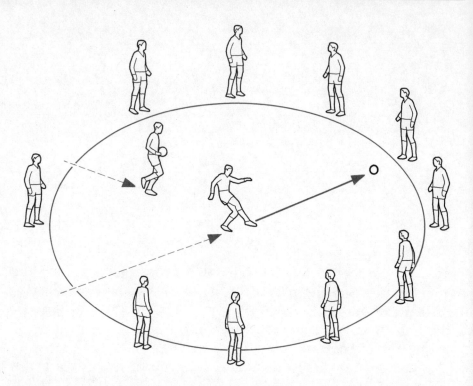

Players form a circle, two of them with footballs. Players dribble or carry the ball to the centre, passing to a colleague before changing places with him.

Variations
1 play a quick one-two
2 turn at the centre, changing direction
3 play a one-two and pass to the next player

Two cones, 20 yards apart, are needed.
The teams are of six players each.

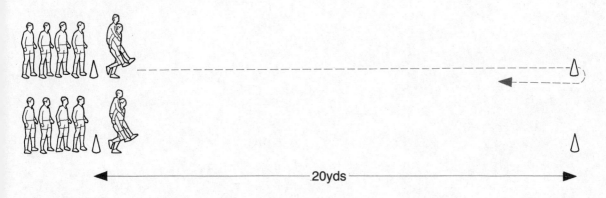

The first player in each team gives a piggy-back to a team-mate.
When the first two players return to the start line, a third player
is carried by two players along the course before returning for
another team-mate to be carried by three players.

All runners must be in contact with the player being carried
and a different player must be carried on each trip.

TECHNIQUE
DRILLS▶

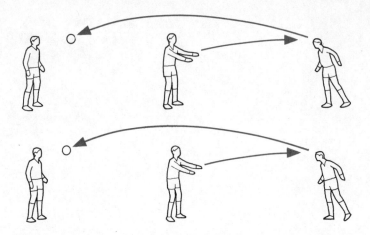

Players are arranged in threes in a single line.

The player in the centre has the ball. He throws it up for the player to head high and firmly to the opposite end player who controls it and returns it to the centre player for him to repeat the exercise.

Variations

1 regularly change the centre player
2 throw the ball up for both standing and jumping headers

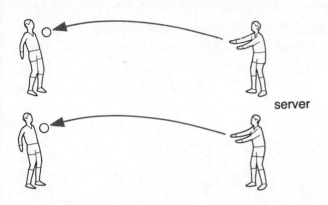

server

Two players, with one ball, face each other. One acts as the server who throws the ball to the chest of his partner. He arches his back to control the ball before allowing it to drop to his feet. He then passes the ball back to the server.

Variation
chest the ball down and
volley back to the server

Two players face one player, 15 yards away. Player (1) passes the ball along the ground and follows the ball to the opposite side, whilst player (2) controls it and passes it to player (3).

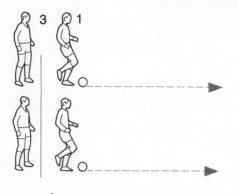

15yds

Variations

1 the passer can run quickly to player (2) to test his control
2 use longer distances for lofted or driven passes

Five players stand on each line, facing each other and 20 yards apart. Three players have a ball; two do not. Two extra players stand in the middle.

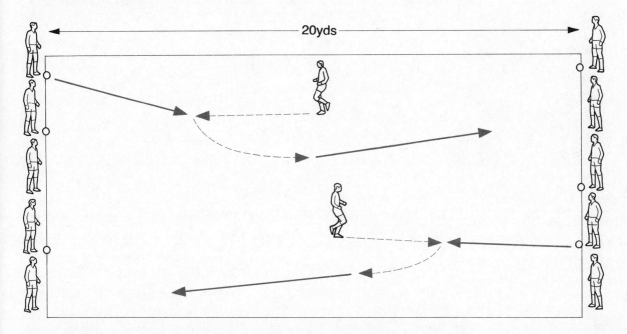

The two players in the middle move towards a player with the ball and demand a pass. When one of these central players receives the ball, he turns and passes to a player on the opposite side who does not have a ball. He then demands a pass from another player and turns to repeat the exercise.

Players must learn to keep their heads up to find the spare player. Work for 30 seconds and change.

Players stand 15 yards apart, with one ball between two.

Players pass the ball with the side of the foot along the ground to the partner facing. Players should be encouraged to move forward to receive the ball, control it and pass it back.

Ensure that the ball is passed on the ground over shorter distances and that players are ready to move towards the ball to collect it and are not caught flat-footed. Stay on your toes and be alert.

Variations
1 increase the distance for a lofted pass
2 shorten the distance for a one-touch pass

A 20-yard square area of play is needed for six players.

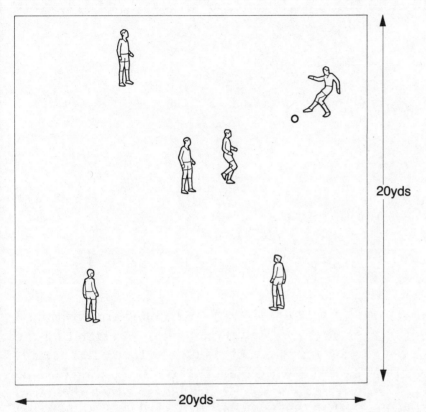

20yds

20yds

Five players have to pass and move within the area and make consecutive passes, 10, 12 or 15 times, without the middle man intercepting. Change the middle man regularly.

Variations
1 make the play two-touch when the players become more confident
2 progress to 4 *v* 2, i.e. with two middle men, within the same area

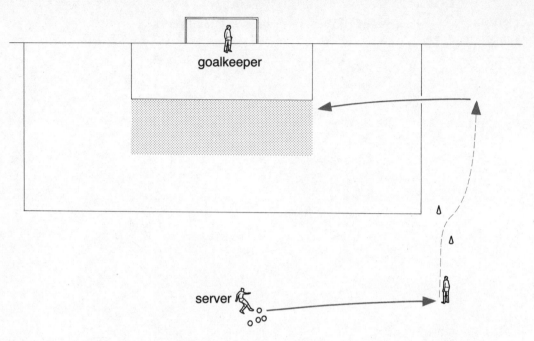

A supply of footballs is required. Two cones are positioned outside the penalty area, with smaller cones extending the length of the six-yard area, but slightly further out. A server supplies the ball to a wide player who attacks the cones as though they were defenders. He dribbles between them and aims to cross the ball into the 'second six-yard area', so as not to make it an easy cross for the goalkeeper to cut out.

Variations

1 as the practice improves, bring in a forward to 'finish' the cross
2 bring in defenders too

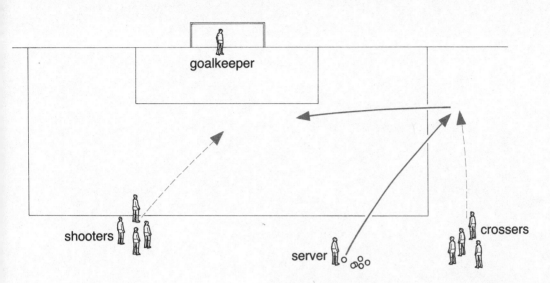

goalkeeper

shooters

server

crossers

The coach acts as server (with a supply of footballs) for this game. The players are in two groups, one of crossers and one of shooters. The coach serves the ball into space for a crosser to run onto and cross first time. Shooters move into the penalty area to anticipate the cross. They should get in a first-time shot at goal if possible.

Variations
1 lofted cross for headers
2 introduce a defender for advanced players

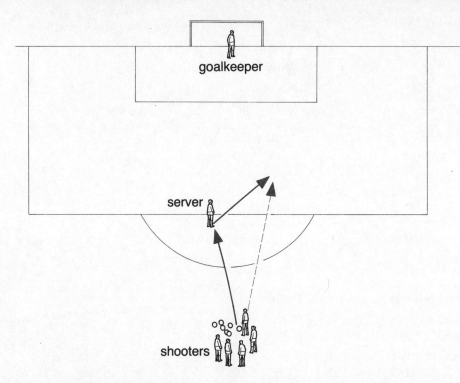

One goal with goalkeeper, and a supply of footballs is needed. Coach acts as server.

One at a time, players pass the ball along the ground to the server who lays it off for the player to follow up with a shot at goal. This encourages accuracy. Players should approach the ball quickly and keep the head still. Get the body over the ball to keep the shot low.

Variation
bounce the ball for volleys, etc.

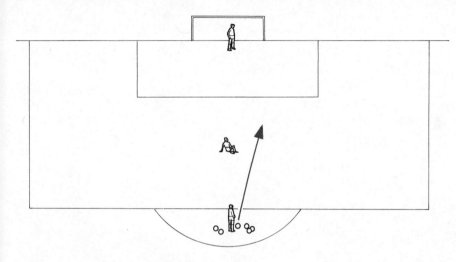

With a supply of footballs in the penalty area, a shooter sits on the penalty spot. The server plays the ball forward for the shooter to get up and shoot from outside the six-yard box before returning to sit down for the next shot.

The shooter has to keep a 'clear' head even though he is shooting whilst tired. Accuracy is essential.

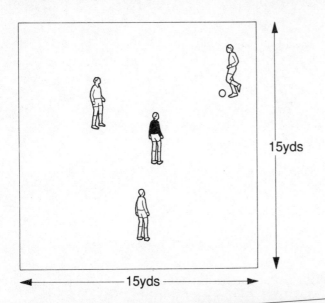

15yds

15yds

An area 15 yards square is needed. Play 3 *v* 1 to a strict time limit of 30 seconds.

The three players have only two or three touches and must be encouraged to pass and move in a tight area. The single player must be encouraged to work hard to win the ball and is rewarded with a 5-second rest if he is successful. A good test for control.

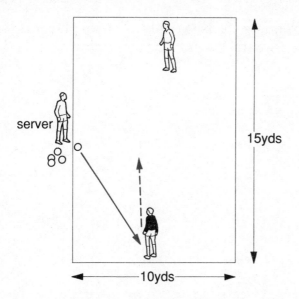

server

15yds

10yds

An area 15 x 10 yards is needed, plus a supply of footballs.

The coach serves the ball to one of two players who has to dribble inside the area to beat his opponent. He scores a point if he is in control of the ball as it goes over the opposite line. Dribbling skills are enhanced.

An area of 15 square yards is required. One player is positioned at three of the corners, leaving one corner free.

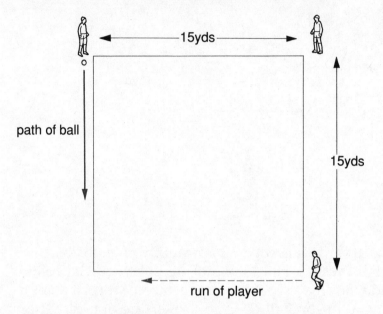

The player in possession of the ball passes it on the floor into the 'free' corner. The player nearest makes a run to the corner and collects the pass. He turns and passes to the space he has left and the next man runs into the space to collect the pass and so on.

Variations
1 go round the other way
2 play two-touch to encourage better body position to turn and pass

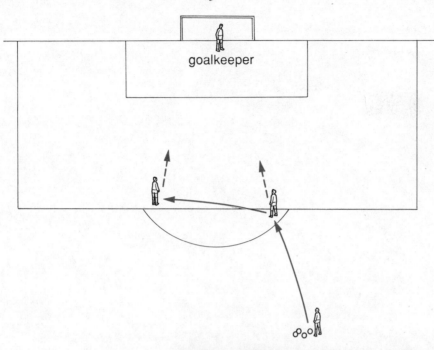

goalkeeper

This takes place in the penalty area and a supply of footballs is needed.

The coach supplies the ball to two strikers who have the choice of turning and shooting or touching the ball on for a partner to shoot.

This encourages quick movement and the non shooters to follow up for rebounds.

Variation
introduce a defender to make forwards think more quickly

'AWARENESS' GAMES ▶

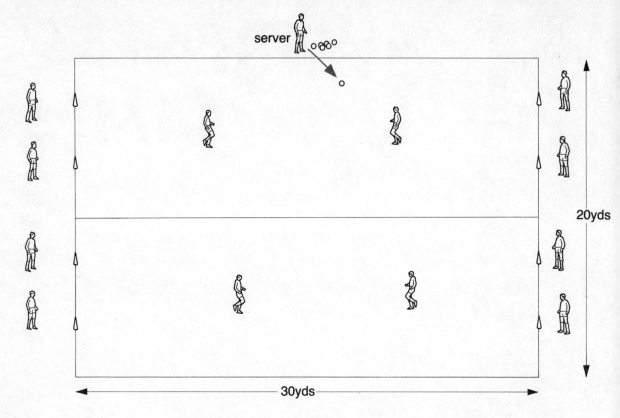

Arrange a 30 x 20 yard area as shown, divided into two pitches with four goals. Two teams play. Players play 1 *v* 1 in their own area but can pass to a colleague on the adjoining pitch.

The coach has a supply of balls to keep the game flowing. Change players often as it can be very tiring.

Variation
score in any goal

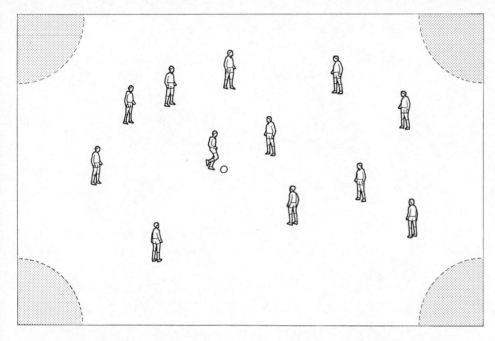

Use small cones to mark the corners of the pitch as shown. Play 6 *v* 6, with the team in possession trying to enter any of the corner areas in possession of the ball. The game encourages players to pass early and run with the ball if they see an area to attack. Urge players to react quickly.

POSSESSION GAME

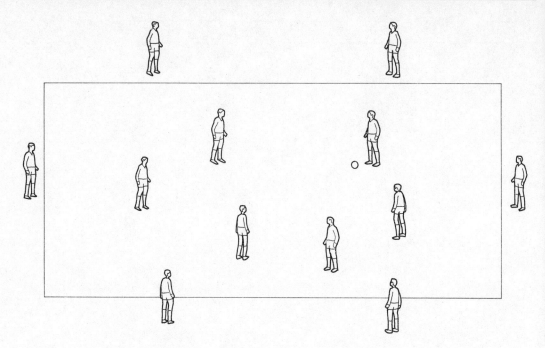

Use the penalty area for 3 *v* 3 game, with other players positioned alternately just outside the area. The aim is to keep possession by using outside players for passing and moving practice. In a 3 *v* 3 game, players should be encouraged to keep their heads up to know where their colleagues are for a passing option.

Variations
1 allow outside players to move to create angles along their line
2 outside players have one or two touches only

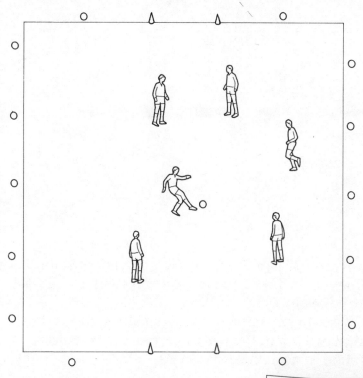

You need a pitch 25 yards square, with two small goals and footballs arranged around the edge of the pitch.

Play 3 *v* 3 to score goals. When the ball goes out of play the team in possession uses the nearest ball to re-start. Encourage quick reactions and quick thinking by all the players.

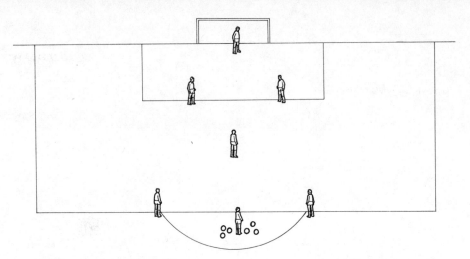

Use six footballs in the penalty area. Two defenders stand on the six-yard line, with three attackers, one on the penalty spot and two on the edge of the 'D'.

The server passes to an attacker on the penalty spot to release defenders and play 3 v 2 in the penalty area. Attackers have to find room for shots at goal. Encourage 'snap' shots.

goalkeeper

One team has a goalkeeper and defends a large goal. The other team has two small goals and attacks a large goal.

One team outnumbers their opponents in the outfield but has two areas to defend. This creates a thinking game and ensures that players are aware of what is going on around them and are not just concentrating on the ball.

Place eight marker cones at random in a large playing area.

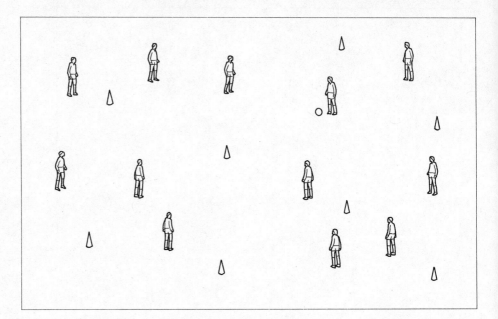

With two teams the object of the game is to hit cones with the ball. Players have to be aware of where the 'free' cones are and change the direction of the play if their chosen cone is defended.

When a cone is hit, play re-starts from the nearest touchline. A game for quick movement and thought.

Put players into three separate teams. The object is for two teams to keep possession from the third team, i.e. the play is 8 *v* 4.

If a player loses possession, then his team become the 'defenders' against the other two teams. The referee or coach needs to work hard to keep up a supply of information on who has lost the ball! The team not in possession should group together and try to win the ball back.

FOUR GOAL GAME

Using eight marker cones, place four goals anywhere in pitch area and play 6 *v* 6.

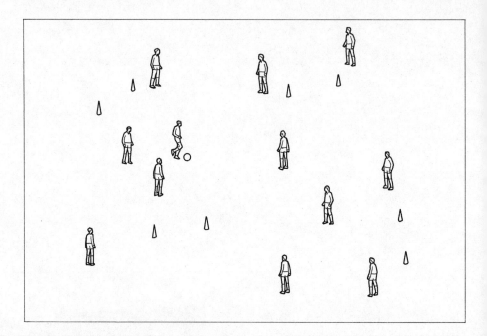

The object is to score in any goal by passing the ball between the goals and below cone height. This encourages players to be aware of areas to attack and be able to change direction when necessary. Encourage players to 'have a go' at passing on the ground when the goals are not defended. When a goal is scored, play re-starts from the nearest touchline.

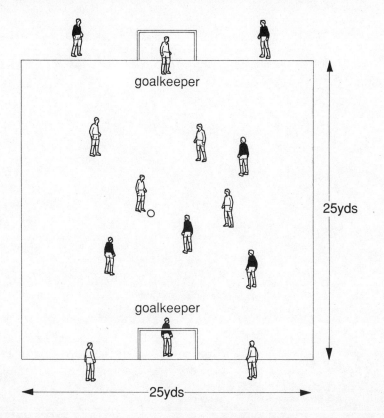

An area 25 yards square is needed with full-size goals and two goalkeepers. A target man is positioned on each side of each goal.

Two teams play 4 *v* 4 but can play off the target men who have one touch to return the ball into play for a possible shot at goal. This game encourages quick thinking and reaction in the goalmouth.

TEAM
GAMES▶

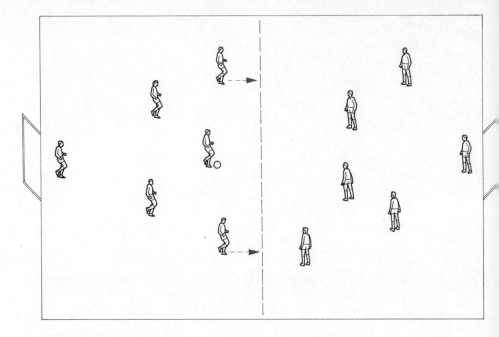

The full pitch area is set up for 6 v 6. Play normally, but all players of one team, excluding the goalkeeper, must be over the half-way line to allow their goals to count.

Variations
1 if any member of the defending side is not in his own half, the goal is doubled!
2 play two-touch football

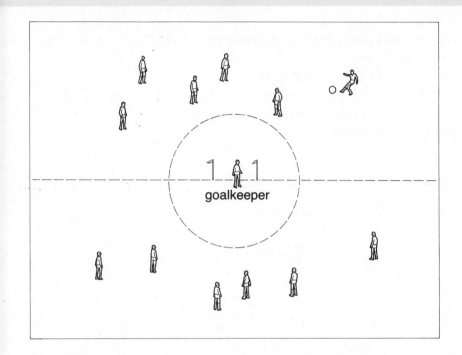

Use a rectangular pitch with a half-way line and a goal set up inside a circle in the centre. Play 3 *v* 3 in each area with the circle a 'no go' area for outfield players. Players should look for shooting opportunities or pass across to team-mates in the other half. Be tactically aware of the best scoring situations.

Use the full pitch area, with two goals and marker lines 10 or 15 yards from the goal. Only the goalkeeper and one target man are allowed in each goal-area.

Play 3 *v* 3 outfield and set up shots after a lay-off from the target man. Encourage the target man to follow shots in for possible rebounds.

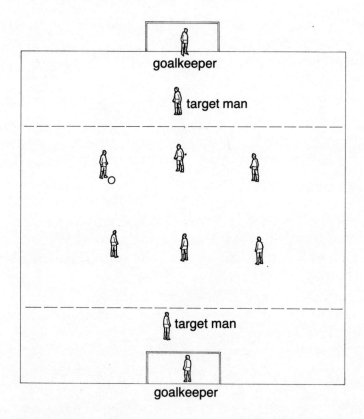

goalkeeper

target man

target man

goalkeeper

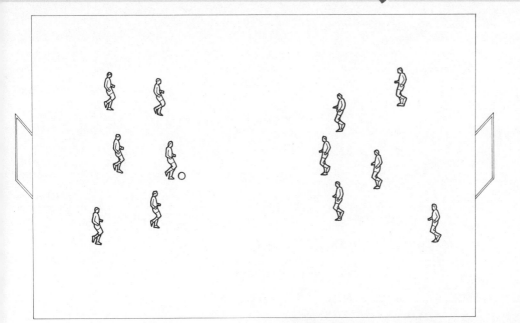

Use a pitch area suitable for 6 *v* 6 game. Put restrictions on players, e.g. no talking or making noises, no use of left foot, or no use of right foot. No free-kicks are awarded for talking etc., but there should be an immediate punishment of ten sit-ups or press-ups, so that a team is momentarily a man short. The coach must keep up with the game!

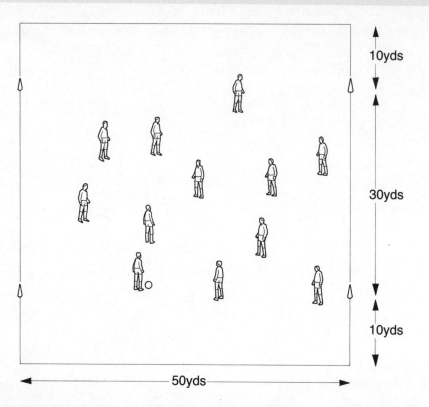

10yds

30yds

10yds

50yds

Place large cones 10 yards in from each touchline and 30 yards apart in the area shown in the diagram. Play 6 *v* 6. The object is to run the ball over the opponents' line between the cones. A player must be in control of the ball when the ball is run. Players can change the direction of the attack as they have a large 'goal' to go for.

Variation

introduce points for passes to encourage the defending team to win the ball back and not just to stay back to defend their line

Two teams of five, in different colours, are needed, as well as two 'spare' players in another colour. 'Spare' players play for the team in possession, making it 7 *v* 5.

Encourage the team without the ball to work hard to win it back. Also the team in possession should not give it away easily. You need to make ten passes to win points.

57

Mark an area for the goalkeeper with small cones. Only the goalkeeper is allowed in this. The object is to chip the ball to your own goalkeeper.

Play 5 *v* 5 outfield. Teams have to make enough space to be able to play a chip or lofted pass to their goalkeeper. They also have to stop their opponents, so they are defending one goal and attacking the other.

Variations
1 pass the ball on the ground
2 use two-touch football for advanced players

Play in an area of about 30 x 15 yards and use marker cones for small goals. Play one-touch football to encourage quick thinking and quick movement. Keep a supply of balls around the area to keep play moving and players alert.

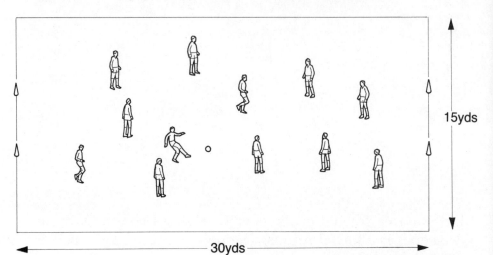

15yds

30yds

Variations
1 introduce goalkeeper
2 play two- or three-touch for younger players

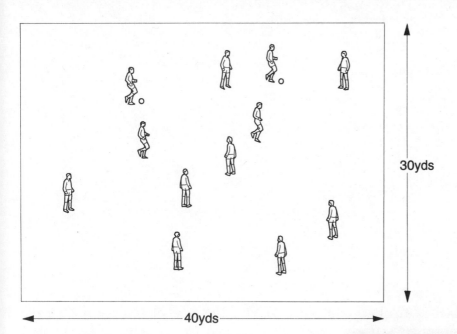

30yds

40yds

Use a pitch area of 40 x 30 yards, with two teams of six players each. Use two footballs of different colours if possible.

Each team has its own ball and tries to keep possession. One team tries to win the other ball, and vice versa.

If one team gains possession of the other ball, the dispossessed team must retrieve their own ball before they can try to win back their opponents' ball.

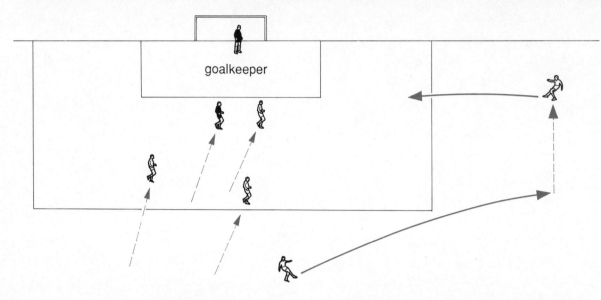

goalkeeper

Each team has one wide player; the rest of the team take up central positions. The ball is passed to the winger for him to take it on and cross.

Three attackers enter the area with one defender. A goal only counts with three or less touches.

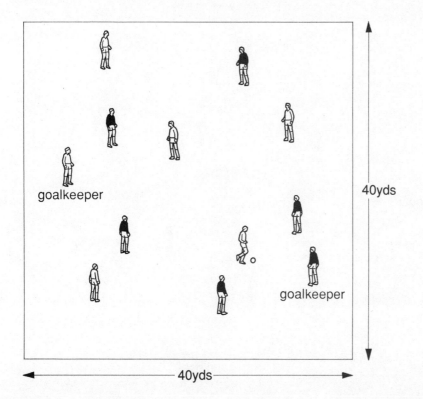

goalkeeper

40yds

goalkeeper

40yds

An area 40 yards square or larger is required. Players are divided into two teams of five plus two goalkeepers. The goalkeepers can move freely in the area. Each team has to keep possession of the ball and scores a point when they pass to either free goalkeeper.

Variations
1 score points for eight passes also, to stop the defending team just marking the goalkeeper
2 assign a goalkeeper to each team

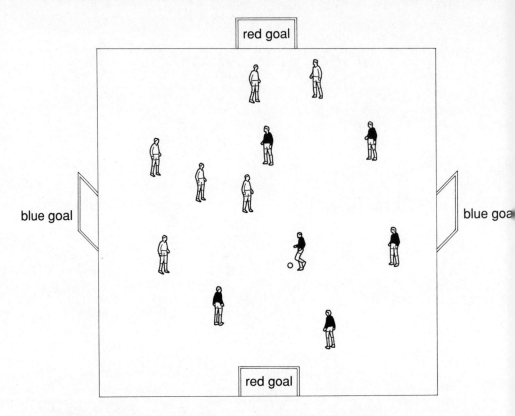

Set up four goals as shown. Players are divided into two teams of six, no goalkeeper, and each team has to defend two goals or attack two goals when in possession.

Players must be able to change direction when in possession and should be encouraged to attack the goal with fewer defenders.

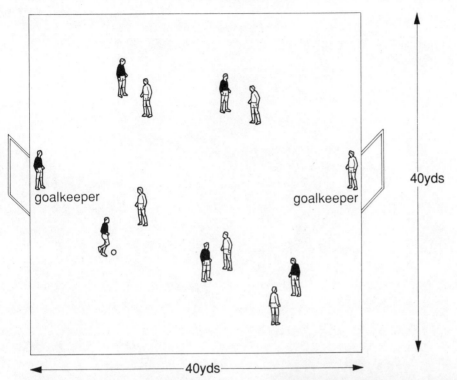

40yds

40yds

goalkeeper   goalkeeper

In an area 40 yards square with two goals and two goalkeepers, the teams play 5 *v* 5. Each player is given a man to mark and is responsible for marking him when opponents have possession and for losing him when his team has the ball.

A good discipline for players.

65

FITNESS GAMES AND RUNS▶

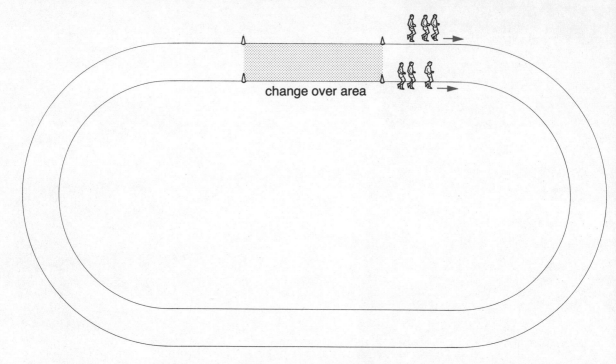

change over area

Two running areas are required, one inside the other. One team runs on the inside with the other on the outside. When a full lap has been run, the teams change tracks between the posts (shaded area). Run for a given length of time (6–10 minutes).

Teams can only change when all the members are between the cones.

Six cones are placed in a straight line at five-yard intervals.

5yds

Player (A) can run to any cone he chooses and Player (B) has to stay with his run. This is timed over 30 seconds.

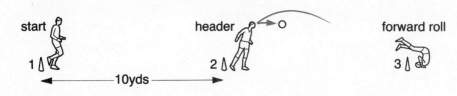

start | header | forward roll | pass and turn
1 | 2 | 3 | 4
10yds

Four cones are placed at 10-yard intervals. A player runs from (1) and is served a header at (2). He runs to (3) and completes a forward roll, is served a short pass at (4), returns it and turns back for a forward roll at (3), a header at (2) and then on to (1). This is timed over 35 seconds.

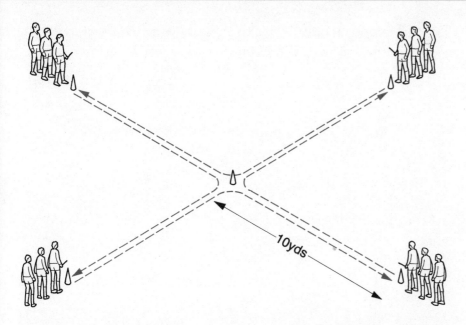

Five cones are needed, one at the centre and others 10 yards away as shown. Use four batons, one for each team. The first player of each team runs to the central cone, touching it with the baton, and checks off to the cone on his right. He checks and runs back to the central cone and then back to the starting cone. This makes a total of 80 yards in one circuit at check and sprint speed.

Play this game penalty area to penalty area, but not with the full width of the pitch. Put goalkeepers in the 'D' at each end.

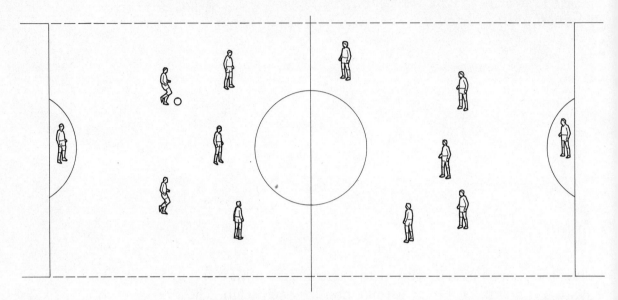

The object is to play 5 *v* 5 on a big pitch and pass the ball to the target man or goalkeeper in the 'D'.

Change the target men every two or three minutes. Play for a set time and get players to work up and down the pitch.

Mark out a circle with cones of any size. For two teams of six each you need five marker cones.

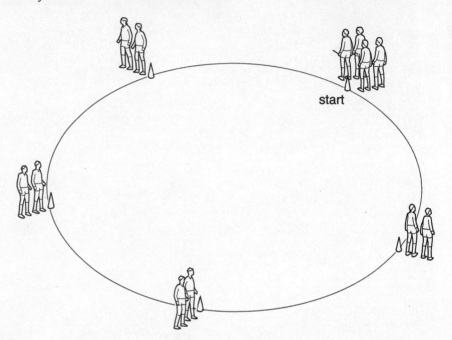

The game is a relay race. Each team has a baton and the race can continue for 6, 12 or 15 minutes. Markers can be placed at different distances to change the length of the run. This is a good test for sprint speed and concentration at take-overs.

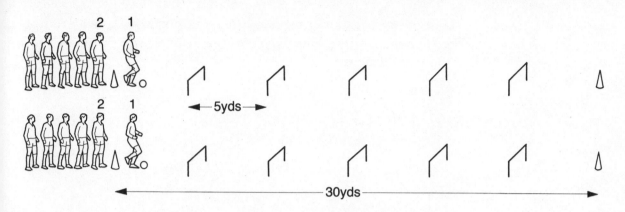

Set up a 30-yard course with hurdles at every five yards.

Player (1) has to run the course, pushing the ball under the hurdle whilst jumping over it himself, through to the end cone and back before handing over to player (2). This will improve fitness and provide interest and competition at the same time.

Variations
1 player may carry the ball and just jump the hurdles
2 players may dribble in and out and hurdle back or jump two hurdles out and dribble back

Use a 30-yard square area, with players positioned as shown to create a dribbling course. Arrange four teams, one at each corner of the area.

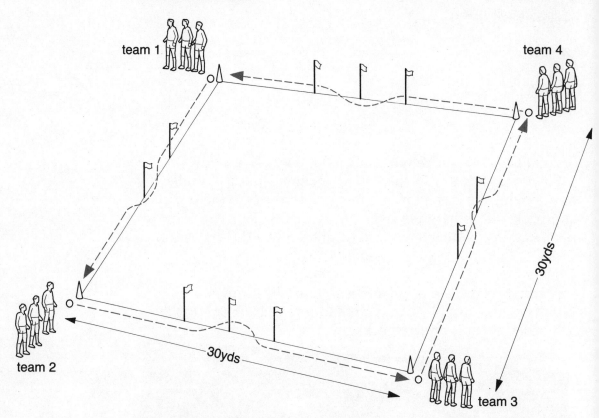

The object is to dribble the ball around the course between the sticks (as shown) and then back to the starting place before passing on to the second player. Dribbling whilst in competition increases concentration. For less skilled or younger players the same course can be used without competition. Encourage control to build confidence.

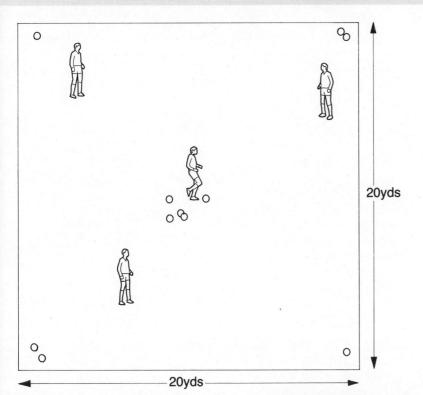

20yds

20yds

This is for four players in an area 20 yards square. Place a supply of footballs in centre. Each player must collect as many balls in his corner as possible. He can 'steal' a ball from opponents if he wishes.

Time the competition or have the first player with four balls declared the winner.

77

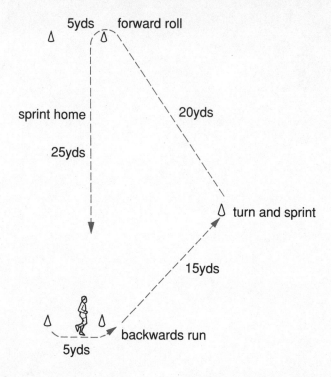

Set up a small course as shown with marker cones and split the group into two teams for sprint races. This exercise incorporates sprints, turns, rolls and competition.

The first runner in team A runs the five-yard distance to the first cone, touching it before turning. He then runs backwards at an angle over 15 yards before turning to sprint to the 20-yard cone. Then a forward roll and through the end 'gate' to sprint home which is the signal for the next runner in the team to go.

The other team competes in the opposite direction.

Set up the course as shown, with 35 yards as a maximum length.

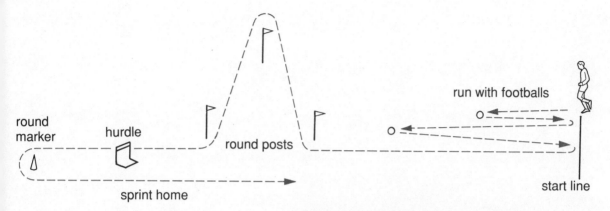

round marker   hurdle   round posts   run with footballs   start line

sprint home

The player has to place two footballs one at a time in a marked area, returning to the start before going on to run round the three posts without touching and on to the small hurdle completing 10 double jumps. The player then goes round the end marker and sprints to the finish or sets off a team mate.

Variations
1 team relay race for competition
2 repeat for three or more runs per player

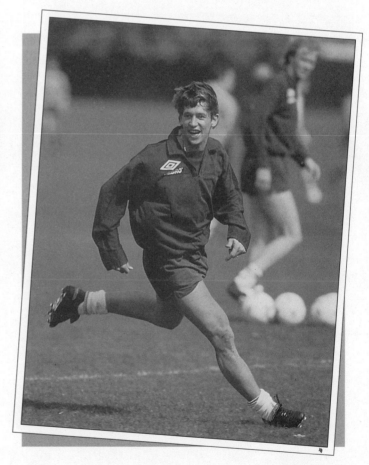